Air Fryer Cook

for Beginners

Full-Coloured Book with Beautiful Pictures for Every Recipes. Prepare Delicious Dishes for Family and Friends

Erin Cox

TABLE OF CONTENTS

INTRODUCTION

Air fryers have started to become popular, due to the fact that you can avoid many of the unhealthy aspects of modern cooking. But what is an air fryer exactly, and how on earth does it work?

Air fryers are basically an upgraded, enhanced countertop oven, but they became popular for one particular reason. In fact, many of the manufacturers, such as Philips, market this machine solely based on the claim that the air fryers accurately mimic deep-frying, which, although extremely unhealthy, is still very popular in this day and age (as it is, in my opinion, one of the most delicious ways to eat food).

Air fryers work with the use of a fan and a heating mechanism. You place the food you want cooked in a basket or on the rack, turn on the machine, and the air fryer distributes oven-temperature hot air around your food. It provides consistent, pervasive heat evenly to all the food within. This heat circulation achieves the crispy taste and texture that is so tantalizing in deep fried foods, but without the unhealthy and dangerous oil! Both have been replaced by this miracle machine with hot air and a fan.

ADVANTAGES TO USING AN AIR FRYER

I may have already slipped in a few of the advantages to using an air fryer, but now let's expand a little more on everything an air fryer can do for you. After all, no investment should be made unless it's absolutely worthwhile.

And in truth, the air fryer is very worthwhile. I cannot begin to tell you how the advantages start piling up; this is not just another average appliance that everyone is getting because of a simple trend. People are getting air fryers because of their incredible, numerous, multifaceted benefits.

There are, however, a few notable advantages of using an air fryer, which I'll list below. If you don't know anything else about air fryers, I hope that these will convince you of their worth.

HEALTHIER COOKING

This is perhaps the top benefit that comes with air frying. In a society that really struggles with healthy cooking, we can use all the help we can get. Luckily, air fryers make it easy, all while maintaining many of the factors that make unhealthy food delicious!

Air fryers use very little oil, which is one of the best ways to replace those unhealthy fried foods, like fried chicken, potatoes, and so many others. If you are like me (a lover of deep fried foods) then this is the answer to your dilemma of healthy eating while still enjoying the crispy taste of food!

Do keep in mind that you still need to spray fried foods, such as fish, with a touch of oil to make sure it does get evenly crispy. All in all, however, there is no denying the amount of oils is a whole lot less.

This singular change makes all the difference in the world. Healthy eating has never been easier, as you'll get the same crispy and flavoursome results, with minimal amounts of added oils. You'll even be able to "fry" foods you never were able to before—the possibilities are endless!

SAFER AND EASIER

Nothing scares me more than a hot pot of oil. It is an accident waiting to happen, and getting struck with burning oil splatters is no joke! But this, and its corresponding injuries, is often the price to pay for deep fried foods.

Air fryers are also user-friendly, and this makes a huge difference. You don't have to feel like you are studying for a degree when working with an air fryer. Making dinner is far less complicated in an air fryer than many of the traditional methods of cooking. For some meals—unless you choose one of the more complex recipes I'll share later—you can even revert to placing a small piece of meat (even if it happens to be frozen!) into the basket and select the cooking settings.

The simplicity of the air fryer is its beauty. You will save countless time and unnecessary frustrations, and still make delicious food!

FASTER THAN COOKING IN THE OVEN

Once you buy an air fryer and set it to heat for the first time, you won't know what hit you! The average normal oven needs about 10 minutes to preheat. Due to the air fryer's smaller size and innovative design, it will be ready to go in no time!

It's even faster during the actual cooking. With the circulation that allows your food to be cooked crisp and even, it cuts a whole lot of cooking time out of the equation. This is amazing, especially in this day and age where technology, work, friends, family, and even pets are constantly demanding our attention.

Just imagine! You could set your food in the air fryer, and (with some recipes) it will be ready to eat in less than 20 minutes!

SAVES SPACE

If you are someone living in a small apartment, or a student accommodation, then an air fryer is perfect for you. Air fryers are much smaller in comparison to a conventional oven and you can easily make use of this air fryer in 1 cubic foot of your kitchen.

You can even pack your air fryer away after use if need be, but the majority of people choose to keep it out on the counter. But it's nice to have the option to move your air fryer around if space becomes an issue.

LOW OPERATING COSTS

Considering how much cooking oil costs these days and the amount you need to use, you will soon be cutting costs in making deep fried foods. All an air fryer uses is a small amount of oil and some of the electricity to power up the air fryer, about the same amount that a countertop oven would.

Not only will you be cutting out the massive oil costs, which will save money, you will likely also save money by ordering out less, as you'll be able to replicate your favourite foods quickly and easily at home!

NO OIL SMELL

In reality, smelling like the food you just ate is not impressive, regardless of how delicious the food may be. This is what often happens, however, when people enjoy deep fried foods.

When deep frying foods, it also causes the whole house to smell, and as the oil splatters around, it can leave a massive mess. The oil can even harden on the walls, causing grime to build up into a nasty concentration of dirt and grease.

With less cooking oil, air fryers don't have any of those oil smells and keeps the space cleaner around you, as all the oils, smells, and actual cooking are contained within the machine.

PRESERVES NUTRIENTS

When you are cooking your food in an air fryer, it actually protects a lot of the food from losing all its moisture. This means that with the use of a little oil, as well as circulation with hot air, it can allow your food to keep most of its nutrients which is excellent for you!

If you want to cook healthy foods with the purpose of maintaining as many nutrients as possible, then an air fryer is perfect for you!

EASIER TO CLEAN

Cleaning is perhaps the bane of my existence, especially after cooking and having a long day. This can really take away a lot of the pleasure of making yourself a great meal. But an air fryer lightens the burden by being easy to clean!

Consistent cleaning after using it (much like any pot or pan) can allow for easier and simpler living. You just need some soapy water and a non-scratch sponge to clean both the exterior and the interior of your air fryer. Some air fryers are even dishwasher-safe!

GREAT FLAVOUR

The flavour of air fryer "fried" foods is nearly identical to traditional frying, and the texture is exact. You can cook a lot of those great frozen foods, such as onion rings or french fries, and still achieve that crunchy effect. This certainly can help you turn to healthier foods, especially if your goal is for healthy but quality meals.

The air fryer helps to cook your food to perfect crispness, instead of the soggy mess that happens when you try alternative methods of cooking foods that are meant to be deep fried (like chicken tenders). No one really enjoys mushy food. The air fryer keeps that desired element while remaining healthy.

All you will really need is just some cooking oil sprayed outside of your food to end up with a cooked interior and a crunchy exterior. So no worries! You still can eat your foods with a crunch and a healthier result!

VERSATILE

Unlike rice cookers meant just for rice, or bread makers meant just for bread, you will find that an air fryer leaves a lot of room to be both versatile and healthier. You can cook almost anything you would like in the air fryer (as long as it fits). From spaghetti squash, to desserts, even to fried chicken!
You will probably never run out of air frying options!

VARIOUS TYPES OF AIR FRYERS AND HOW TO CHOOSE THE ONE FOR YOU

There isn't one standardized choice of air fryers, which means you are far more likely to find an air fryer that really suits your particular needs. Whether it be size or price, you have a wider variety of choices than what normally comes with conventional ovens.

So what are the key aspects that you need to take into consideration when getting yourself a nice air fryer? Let's begin:

- **Dimensions:** Obviously they come in different sizes, and despite saving space, some can still be bulky. When thinking about your countertop, you do want to consider its size and dimensions. You don't want to play a game of tilt with your air fryer, nor have it taken up all the extra space you have!

- **Safety Features:** You may want to check that it has an auto shutoff, as it is certainly a desirable feature. Air fryers can get very hot during use, and an auto-shutoff can save you a lot of stress and fire emergencies. Furthermore, having a cool exterior can prevent potential red and burnt hands. So do yourself a favour and make sure they have all these elements at hand.

- **Reviews:** Naturally, this is the best thing to check out. Considering that the businesses rarely give out all the information, you will certainly find it out when people leave reviews. The customer hides nothing, and if they are unhappy, they make sure everyone else knows about it. However, if people are very happy, many of them will also note it in the reviews, and it is best to target the air fryers that tend to have the high reviews.

TWO COMMON DIFFERENCES

Beyond those functional differences, there are two mainstream designs of air fryers: basket air fryers and oven air fryers. Each has very unique and distinguished features in which to enjoy. Let us take a look at the differences between the two:

BASKET AIR FRYERS

Basket fryers are known to need less space than oven air fryers, which is very practical if you have limited space. Not only does it save space, but it also saves time, as the food is quickly heated up (without unnecessarily heating up the kitchen). Unlike an oven air fryer, and the larger traditional oven, it only takes about 1-2 minutes for the basket air fryer to heat up, and it is quite easy to place the foods inside of the basket.

The cons are, for one, that it does make a lot more noise than the oven air fryer. You also will not be able to watch the food as it cooks, which can increase the chances of burnt food if you are not careful. Also, a basket air fryer may not be the best if you need to cook a lot of food, as it is limited in capacity. This means that batch cooking may be required if you need a large amount of food.

This makes a basket air fryer ideal if you have a limited budget, don't need to cook a huge amount of food, and have limited free time. They are quick, small, and convenient, especially perfect for people who are students or single working professionals, and maybe even you!

OVEN AIR FRYERS

Oven air fryers, in contrast, have a larger capacity, which means you can cook a lot more food at the same time. They also have multiple functions for cooking and cut down on the noise than the basket air fryer. You will also be able to move the food closer or even further away from the heating element. There is a lot more flexibility involved in the use of an oven air fryer. Best of all, you can place parts of the oven air fryer into the dishwasher to be washed (thus cutting down the cleaning process, if you happen to have a dishwasher).

But, do be aware that it takes up more counter space, and takes a larger initial bite out of your wallet. It may also heat up the kitchen more, and if you are in fashion and aesthetic design, it might be disappointing to find out the colours and themes are more limited than basket air fryers.

These are the two main common types of air fryers; however, there are new types of air fryers that are coming to light for you to use and enjoy, most notably, the paddle-type air fryer. This version has a paddle that moves through the basket of your air fryer in order to help circulate hot air in between each piece of food.

This saves you the effort of pulling your food out at a specific time and shaking or stirring it. These can also be noisy, and heat up the space, and are not small and convenient; however, if you are someone looking for convenience, then this is the air fryer to go for.

ACCESSORY TOOLS FOR AIR FRYER COOKING

I love how air fryers save time, so I've compiled a list of my favourite time-saving tools that I often use when meal prepping with my air fryer. Anything to help make your life easier and healthier should certainly be considered, and what better way to help than by adding some accessories to your air fryer inventory?

MANDOLINE

Preparation is always needed before jumping into air frying, and getting yourself the mandoline slicer is the perfect tool to slice online rings, pickles, or even the best and crunchiest chips. You can select the thickness or thinness, depending on what the recipe needs and says, so you will always be able to get the perfect crispness.

GRILL PAN

This is simply a pan created with a perforated surface. With this tool, you can both grill and sear foods like fish or even vegetables inside your air fryer. They are also commonly non-stick, which really helps your overall clean-up.

However, before you purchase a grill pan, make sure the air fryer model you have does support the grill pan. The last thing you want is to find that your grill pan just does not fit inside your air fryer.

HEAT RESISTANT TONGS

There is no denying how hot an air fryer can get inside, and unless you are a superhero, you will need some help manoeuvring in foods in and outside of the basket if need be. Using heat-resistant tongs can really make your life infinitely easier by keeping your foods, and your hands, safe. They are affordable, and really useful to allow for an even cooking process.

AIR FRYER LINERS

If you'd like to further decrease your clean-up time, then this is for you! These liners are both non-stick and non-toxic, making this a classic little investment for you to consider. They prevent the food from sticking to your air fryer and help in the process of keeping your little machine clean. You will not have to worry about burnt foods inside your fryer again!

AIR FRYER RACK

This adds a little bit more versatility as you can really take advantage of the surface cooking. With a rack, you ensure that heat is evenly distributed to all 360 degrees of your food. They are very safe and easy to use, and they increase the number of dishes you can cook at the same time

BAKING PANS

With an air fryer, you can even bake! You just need the right equipment, such as a barrel or round pan. With this you can even bake pizza, bread, muffins, and more. Imagine telling people you baked your own cake with an air fryer!

SILICONE BAKING CUPS

From egg bites to muffins, these are individual cups you can use in order to help compensate for the smaller space within an air fryer. The silicone material is heat-resistant, and allows for easier release of the contents, which spares you a lot of time cleaning. If you are a fan of baking, then this is a must have.

OIL SPRAYER

Naturally, one of the top benefits is needing much less oil when cooking with an air fryer, but it does not necessarily mean that you can cook with no oil at all. An oil sprayer is the key to getting the food you want to that nice golden-brown. You can use any oil that you like to use when cooking; all you need is a little spritz before you close the machine, and you are set!

THERMAPEN

Having the right cooking time is very important, but temperature also counts for a lot, and this is a nice little accessory to add to your collection. Having an instant-read thermometer can ensure all the food you have is cooked (and evenly so). If you are not completely certain at what temperatures food should be, you can always check out the various different guides.

HOW TO CLEAN AN AIR FRYER

As mentioned before, an air fryer is really easy to clean, but that doesn't mean you'll never need to clean it! Also, please remember that the cleanliness of your machine depends on how often you use it, and what you use it for.

It is recommended that you clean your air fryer after every use. As tempting as it may be to skip a day, it really is not worth it over the long run.
And that is the first step that comes with cleaning an air fryer:

- Do not delay the cleaning. Simply don't. Allowing crumbs or random bits of food to harden overnight can turn an easy task into a nightmare of a chore. If you do happen to air-fry foods that come with a form of sticky sauce, then the warmer they are, the easier again they will be to clean and remove.

- Unplug the machine, and use warm and soapy water to properly remove the dirt and components. You do not want anything abrasive in there. If there is food that gets stuck, try soaking it until it is soft enough to remove.

- If there is any food that happens to be stuck on the grate or in the basket, then you should consider gently using a toothpick or even a wooden skewer to scrape it off, in order to be thorough with your cleaning process.

- Remember to wipe the inside with a damp, soapy cloth, and remember to remove both the drawer and the basket.

- Finally, wipe the outside of your air fryer with a damp cloth or a sponge.

If there are any odors that seem to be stuck to your air fryer after cooking a strong food, even after you have cleaned it, then you can consider using a product called NewAir.

Just soak it in with water for about 3o minutes to an hour before you clean it. If the smell remains, then rub one lemon half over the drawer and the basket. Allow it to soak for another 30 minutes before washing it again.

Please do be careful with any non-stick appliances. They are a wonder for cleaning, but they can flake or come off over time. Be gentle, as you do not want anything to scratch or to even chip the coating. Not only does it ruin a little bit of the aesthetic look, a small part of your air fryer will constantly be struggling with sticky food.

There you have it! The first stepping stones and foundational knowledge of an air fryer. The device you will choose, and how you will use it is up to you, but there are still so many exciting varieties, choices, and options to come!

SCRAMBLED EGGS

5 minutes

15 minutes

2

INGREDIENTS

- 4 large eggs
- 2 tbsp unsalted butter, melted
- 65 grams of shredded sharp Cheddar cheese

DIRECTIONS

1. Crack eggs into a round baking dish and whisk. After that, put the dish into the air fryer basket.
2. Set the temperature to 200 C and set the timer for 10 min.
3. After 5 min, stir the eggs and add the butter and cheese. Let cook 3 more min and stir again.
4. Allow eggs to finish cooking an additional 2 min or remove if they are to your desired liking.
5. Use a fork to fluff. Serve warm.

Nutrition: Calories: 359; Protein: 19.5 g; Fibre: 0.0 g; Fat: 27.6 g; Carbohydrates: 1.1 g; Sugar: 0.5 g

FRIED BACON

2 minutes

8 minutes

3

INGREDIENTS

- 1 pack Back Bacon

DIRECTIONS

1. Place the bacon slices in a single layer of the air fryer tray or in the basket.
2. Cook for 8 - 10 minutes at 200°C. There is no need to preheat
3. Depending on the thickness of the bacon the cooking time may vary, so check as you go along whether it is cooked to the point you want

Nutrition: Calories: 118kcal; Protein: 21g; Fat: 4g

BUTTERMILK BISCUITS

5 minutes

18 minutes

16 biscuits

INGREDIENTS

- 190 grams of all-purpose flour
- 1 tbsp baking powder
- 1 tsp kosher salt
- 1 tsp sugar
- ½ tsp baking soda
- 130 grams of buttermilk, chilled
- 8 tbsp unsalted butter, at room temperature

DIRECTIONS

1. Stir together the flour, baking powder, salt, sugar and baking soda in a large bowl.
2. Add the butter and stir to mix well. Pour in the buttermilk and stir with a rubber spatula just until incorporated.
3. Place the dough onto a lightly floured surface and roll the dough out to a disk, 12 mm thick. Cut out the biscuits with a 5 cm round cutter and re-roll any scraps until you have 16 biscuits.
4. Arrange the biscuits in the air fryer basket in a single layer.
5. Place the basket on the bake position.
6. Select Bake, set temperature to 163 degs C, and set time to 18 min.
7. When cooked, the biscuits will be golden brown.
8. Remove from the air fryer grill to a plate and serve hot.

Nutrition: Calories 125; Fat 6.7 g; Carbohydrates 10.7 g; Sugar 3.5 g; Protein 5.2 g

SAUSAGES IN AIR FRYER

5 minutes

12 minutes

6

INGREDIENTS

- 6 Sausages
- 3 squirts Spray Oil

DIRECTIONS

1. Preheat your air fryer to 180°C for 5 minutes
2. Prick each sausage a couple of times (you can use a knife or fork).
3. Spray the bottom of the air fryer with a few splashes of oil to prevent the sausages from sticking.
4. Use the tongs to gently insert the sausages (do not let them touch so that they cook evenly).
5. Set timer to 12 minutes (adjust the time for small, large or frozen sausages).
6. Halfway through cooking, turn with tongs.
7. Check after 12 minutes and reheat if necessary.Serve with your chosen meal

Nutrition: Calories: 209kcal; Carbohydrates: 2g; Protein: 11g; Fat: 17g

SCOTCH EGGS

15 minutes

12 minutes

6

INGREDIENTS

- 6 boiled eggs peeled
- 1 packet 400g Powters Sausagemeat
- 30 g Flour
- ½ teaspoon garlic powder
- 1 large egg beaten
- 120 g Breadcrumbs
- 1 tablespoon brown sugar
- ½ smoked paprika

DIRECTIONS

1. Divide the sausage into 6 equal portions and roll them into a balls
2. Place a sausage ball on your counter or parchment paper if you don't want to clean up later.
3. Pat the sausage balls until they reach the form of an oval big enough to hold an egg.
4. Place the peeled, boiled eggs in the center of the sausages patties and wrap the sausages around the eggs, applying pressure with your hands.
5. Now take 3 bowls and put, in order: flour and garlic powder combined, beaten egg, panko or breadcrumbs with brown sugar and smoked paprika.
6. Roll each sausage-covered egg in bowl 1, then dip in bowl 2 and coat in the breadcrumbs bowl.
7. Preheat your air fryer to 190°C for 10 minutes.
8. Place Scotch eggs in the air fryer basket, ensuring enough space between each other to let the air circulate.
9. Air fry the eggs for 12 minutes, evenly turning halfway through to brown.

Nutrition: Calories 396; Fat 27 g; Protein 29 g; Carbs 16 g; Fiber 1 g; Sugar 1 g

CHEESY PANCAKE

10 minutes

8 minutes

2

INGREDIENTS

- 5 eggs, beaten
- 30 grams almond flour
- ½ tsp baking powder
- 1 tsp apple cider vinegar
- 30 grams Cheddar cheese, shredded
- 1 tsp butter
- 1 tbsp mascarpone
- ½ tsp sesame oil

DIRECTIONS

1. Brush the air fryer basket with sesame oil. Then in the mixing bowl mix up all remaining ingredients. Stir the liquid until homogenous. Pour it in the air fryer pan and place it in the air fryer. Cook the pancake for 8 minutes at 182 degs C.
2. Remove the cooked pancake from the air fryer pan and cut it into servings.

Nutrition: Calories: 276; Fat: 21.4g; Fibre: 0.4g; Carbs: 2.6g; Protein:19g

LEMON AND ALMOND COOKIES

10 minutes

8 minutes

4

INGREDIENTS

- 4 tbsp coconut flour
- ½ tsp baking powder
- 1 tsp lemon juice
- ¼ tsp vanilla extract
- ¼ tsp lemon zest, grated
- 2 eggs, beaten
- 30 ml of organic almond milk
- 1 tsp avocado oil
- ¼ tsp Himalayan pink salt

DIRECTIONS

1. In the big bowl mix up all ingredients from the list above. Knead the soft dough and cut it into 4 pieces. Preheat the air fryer to 200 degs C. Then line the air fryer basket with baking paper.
2. Roll the dough pieces in the balls and press them gently to get the shape of flat cookies. Place the cookies in the air fryer and cook them for 8 minutes.

Nutrition: Calories: 74; Fat: 3.8g; Fibre: 3.1g; Carbs: 5.6g; Protein:4.4g

GRILLED CHEESE SANDWICH

5 minutes

5 minutes

1

INGREDIENTS

- 2 slices of bread
- 2 slices of turkey
- 2 slices of cheddar
- 15 grams of butter

DIRECTIONS

1. Preheat the air fryer to 180 degs C.
2. Spread the butter on the slices of bread.
3. Place the turkey and cheese slices on a slice of bread.
4. Cover the sandwich with the other slice of bread.
5. Place the sandwich in the basket of the air fryer and cook for 5 minutes.
6. Serve and enjoy your meal

Nutrition: Calories: 546; Fat: 28 g; Fibre: 1 g; Carbs: 36 g; Protein: 32 g

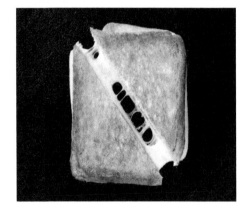

BANANA MUFFIN

10 minutes

10 minutes

12

INGREDIENTS

- 1 egg
- 250 grams of all-purpose flour
- 80 grams of butter, melted
- 1 teaspoon of cinnamon
- 150 grams of sugar
- 3 bananas, mashed
- 1 teaspoon of baking soda
- 1 teaspoon of baking powder
- 1/2 teaspoon of salt

DIRECTIONS

1. Preheat the air fryer to 180 degs C.
2. Put all the ingredients in a blender and blend them until well blended.
3. Pour the batter into the silicone muffin molds.
4. Place the muffin tins in the air fryer basket and cook for 10 minutes.
5. Serve and enjoy your breakfast!

Nutrition: Calories: 189; Fat: 6 g; Fibre: 2 g; Carbs: 20 g; Protein: 10 g; Sugar: 12g

CHOCOLATE PUDDING

15 minutes

10 minutes

2

INGREDIENTS

- 60 ml of butter
- 60 ml of whole milk
- 120 grams of chocolate chips, melted
- 1 egg
- 4 tablespoons of sugar
- Spray oil, for greasing
- 240g of flour

DIRECTIONS

1. Take a bowl and put the butter in it.
2. Melt it by putting it in the microwave.
3. Mix well and add the sugar and milk.
4. At the end, add egg and flour.
5. Incorporate the melted chocolate chips.
6. Pour this mixture into greased molds.
7. Place the molds in the basket of the air fryer and cook for 10 minutes at 40 degs C.
8. When ready, serve and enjoy.
9. The internal consistency will be liquid.

Nutrition: Calories: 800; Fat: 46 g; Protein: 31 g; Carbs: 64 g; Fibre: 4 g; Sugar: 36 g

AVOCADO TOAST

12 minutes

10 minutes

2

INGREDIENTS

- 1 large avocado, pitted
- 1 tablespoon of lemon juice
- Salt to taste.
- A pinch of paprika
- 2 slices of cereal bread
- 1 tablespoon of butter
- 2 eggs
- Spray oil, for greasing

DIRECTIONS

1. The first step is to pit the avocados and put them in a bowl, then add the lemon juice, paprika and salt.
2. Spread the butter on the bread and spread the avocado puree on the other slice.
3. Place the bread, butter side down, into the basket of the air fryer.
4. Cook for 10 minutes at 175 degs C.
5. Meanwhile, break the eggs into a pan and cook them in butter if desired, then serve over the toast.
6. Enjoy your meal.

Nutrition: Calories: 270; Fat: 20 g; Protein: 8.5 g; Carbs: 11 g; Fibre: 5 g; Sugar: 0 g

CRISPY SPICED POTATOES

10 minutes

20 minutes

4

INGREDIENTS

- 900 grams of baby red potatoes, quartered
- 2 tbsp extra-virgin olive oil
- 35 grams dried onion flakes
- 1 tsp dried rosemary
- 1/2 tsp onion powder
- 1/2 tsp garlic powder
- 1/4 tsp celery powder
- 1/4 tsp freshly ground black pepper
- 1/2 tsp dried parsley
- 1/2 tsp sea salt

DIRECTIONS

1. Place the crisper tray on the air fry position. Select Air Fry, set the temperature to 199 degs C, and set the time to 20 min.
2. Meanwhile, place all the ingredients in a large bowl and toss until evenly coated.
3. Add the potatoes to the crisper tray. Air fry for 10 min.
4. After 10 min, shake the crisper tray well. Place the crisper tray back in the grill to resume cooking.
5. After 10 min, check for desired crispness. Continue cooking up to 5 min more, if necessary.

Nutrition: Calories 217; Fat 7 g; Carbohydrates 36 g; Protein 4 g; Fibre 4 g; Sugar 3 g

BRUSCHETTA WITH TOMATO AND BASIL

5 minutes

6 minutes

6

INGREDIENTS

- 4 tomatoes, diced
- 45 grams of shredded fresh basil
- 30 grams shredded Parmesan cheese
- 1 tbsp balsamic vinegar
- 1 tbsp minced garlic
- 1 tsp olive oil
- 1 tsp salt
- 1 tsp freshly ground black pepper
- 1 loaf French bread, cut into 2-cm-thick slices
- Cooking Spray

DIRECTIONS

1. Place the crisper tray on the bake position. Select Bake, set the temperature to 121 degs C, and set the time to 3 min.
2. Get a bowl and mix in the tomatoes, basil, cheese, vinegar, garlic, olive oil, salt and pepper until well incorporated. Set aside.
3. Spritz the crisper tray with cooking spray. Working in batches, lay the bread slices in the crisper tray in a single layer. Spray the slices with cooking spray.
4. Bake for 3 min until golden brown.
5. Remove from the crisper tray to a plate. Repeat with the remaining bread slices.
6. Top each slice with a generous spoonful of the tomato mixture and serve.

Nutrition: Calories 48; Fat 2.3 g; Carbohydrates 6,6 g; Protein 1,3 g; Fibre 0 g; Sugar 4,83 g

CREAMY MASHED POTATOES

5 minutes

25 minutes

4

INGREDIENTS

- 900 baking potatoes (small to medium)
- 40 g butter
- 60 g cream cheese
- 2 stalks of fresh chives
- salt and pepper to taste

DIRECTIONS

1. Start by placing your potatoes into a foil packet, Layout your foil, then place the potatoes in them.
2. Air fry for 25 minutes at 200C. Check after 25 minutes if they are soft; The actual time will depend on the type of air fryer you have and the size of the potatoes.
3. Use a fork (or a potato masher if you prefer) to mash the potatoes.
4. Put the potatoes in a bowl.
5. Add the cream cheese and butter.
6. Add the chives and continue to mix. Continue mixing until the potatoes are mashed and the cream cheese and butter are combined.
7. Plate, serve and enjoy!

Nutrition: Calories: 322; Sugar: 3 g; Fat: 11 g; Carbohydrates: 50 g; Fiber: 5 g; Protein: 7 g

CRISPY AVOCADO CHIPS

15 minutes

10 minutes

4

INGREDIENTS

- 1 egg
- 1 tbsp lime juice
- 1/8 tsp hot sauce
- 2 tbsp flour
- 95 grams of panko breadcrumbs
- 30 grams cornmeal
- 1/4 tsp salt
- 1 large avocado, pitted, peeled, and cut into 1.2 cm slices
- Cooking Spray

DIRECTIONS

1. Whisk together the egg, hot sauce, and lime juice in a small bowl.
2. Place now the flour on a sheet of wax paper. In a separate sheet of wax paper, combine the cornmeal, breadcrumbs, and salt.
3. Dredge the avocado slices one at a time in the flour, then in the egg mixture, finally roll them in the bread crumb mixture to coat well.
4. Place the breaded avocado slices in the air fry basket and mist them with cooking spray.
5. Place the basket on the air fry position.
6. Select Air Fry, set to 199 degs C, and set time to 10 min.
7. When cooking is complete, the slices should be nicely browned and crispy. Transfer the avocado slices to a plate and serve.

Nutrition: Calories 232; Fat 10 g; Carbohydrates 27.5 g; Protein 7 g; Fibre 5.5 g; Sugar 3 g

CRISPY COURGETTE ROUNDS

5 minutes

14 minutes

4

INGREDIENTS

- 2 courgettes, sliced into 6.35- to 12.7-mm-thick rounds (about 255 grams)
- 1/4 tsp garlic granules
- 1/8 tsp sea salt
- Freshly ground black pepper, to taste (optional)
- Cooking Spray

DIRECTIONS

1. Spritz the air fry basket with cooking spray.
2. Put the courgette rounds in the air fry basket, spreading them out as much as possible. Top with a sprinkle of sea salt, garlic granules, and black pepper (if desired). Spritz the courgette rounds with cooking spray.
3. Place the basket on the toast position.
4. Select Toast, set temperature to 200 degs C, and set time to 14 min. Flip the courgette rounds halfway through.
5. When cooking is complete, the courgette rounds should be crisp-tender. Remove from the air fryer grill. Let them rest for 5 min and serve.

Nutrition: Calories 75; Fat 3 g; Carbohydrates 12 g; Protein 5 g; Fibre 3 g; Sugar 12 g

FRENCH FRIES

15 minutes

25 minutes

4

INGREDIENTS

- 455 grams Maris Piper or King Edward potatoes, cut in 5 cm strips
- 3 tbsp canola oil

DIRECTIONS

1. Place the potatoes in a bowl and cover them with cold water. Let soak for 30 min. Drain well, then pat with a paper towel until very dry.
2. Place the crisper tray on the air fry position. Select Air Fry, set temp to 199 degs C, and set the time to 25 min.
3. Meanwhile, in a large bowl, toss the potatoes with the oil.
4. Add the potatoes to the crisper tray. Air fry for 10 min.
5. After 10 min, shake the crisper tray well. Place the crisper tray back in the grill to resume cooking.
6. After 10 min, check for desired crispness. Continue cooking up to 5 min more, if necessary. When cooking is complete, you can serve with your favourite dipping sauce.

Nutrition: Calories 169; Fat 10.5 g; Carbohydrates 17 g; Protein 2 g; Fibre 2 g; Sugar 0.3 g

ONION RINGS

10 minutes

10 minutes

3

INGREDIENTS

- 2 white onions, sliced into rings
- 130 grams flour
- 2 eggs, beaten
- 130 grams breadcrumbs

DIRECTIONS

1. Cover the onion rings with flour.
2. Dip in the egg.
3. Dredge with breadcrumbs.
4. Add to the air fryer.
5. Set it to air fry.
6. Cook at 200 degs C for 10 min.

Serving Suggestions: Serve with tartar sauce.

Prep & Cooking Tips: Make ahead of time and freeze.

Air fry when ready to serve.

Nutrition: Calories 415; Fat 7 g; Carbohydrates 66 g; Protein 19 g; Fibre 8 g; Sugar 8.5 g

COURGETTES FRITTERS

10 minutes

10 minutes

4

INGREDIENTS

- 2 courgettes, grated
- 115 grams of blue cheese
- 1 egg, beaten
- 1 tbsp flaxseed
- 1 tsp dried coriander
- ¼ tsp salt
- 30 grams spring onions, chopped
- 1 tsp olive oil
- 85 grams of celery stalk, diced
- 1 tbsp coconut flour

DIRECTIONS

1. Crumble Blue cheese and mix it up with grated courgettes. Add egg, flaxseed, dried coriander, salt, spring onions, diced celery stalk, and coconut flour. Then stir the ingredients with the help of the spoon until homogenous.
2. Make the fritters and sprinkle them with olive oil. After this, preheat the air fryer to 200 degs C.
3. Place the courgette fritters in the air fryer and cook them for 5 minutes. Then flip the fritters on another side and cook for 5 minutes more or until they are golden brown.

Nutrition: Calories: 164; Fat: 11.6g; Fibre: 2.8g; Carbs: 6.9g; Protein:9.6g

BREADED GREEN OLIVES

5 minutes

8 minutes

4

INGREDIENTS

- 155 grams of jar pitted green olives
- 65 grams all-purpose flour
- Salt and pepper, to taste
- 65 grams breadcrumbs
- 1 egg
- Cooking Spray

DIRECTIONS

1. Place the crisper tray on the air fry position. Select Air Fry, set temp to 200 degs C, and set the time to 8 min.
2. Remove the olives from the jar and dry thoroughly with paper towels.
3. In a small bowl, combine the flour with salt and pepper to taste. Place the breadcrumbs in another small bowl. In a third small bowl, beat the egg.
4. Spritz the crisper tray with cooking spray.
5. Dip the olives in the flour, then the egg, and then the breadcrumbs.
6. Place the breaded olives in the crisper tray. It is okay to stack them. Spray the olives with cooking spray. Air fry for 6 min. Flip the olives and air fry for an additional 2 min, or until brown and crisp.
7. Cool before serving.

Nutrition: Calories 185; Fat 7.5 g; Carbohydrates 20 g; Protein 7 g; Fibre 3 g; Sugar 0.7 g

CRISPY PROSCIUTTO-WRAPPED ASPARAGUS

5 minutes

16 to 24 minutes

6

INGREDIENTS

- 12 asparagus spears, woody ends trimmed
- 24 pieces thinly sliced prosciutto
- Cooking Spray

DIRECTIONS

1. Place the crisper tray on the air fry position. Select Air Fry, set the temperature to 182 degs C, and set the time to 4 min.
2. Wrap each asparagus spear with 2 slices of prosciutto, then repeat this process with the remaining asparagus and prosciutto.
3. Spray the crisper tray with cooking spray, then place 2 to 3 bundles in the crisper tray. Air fry for 4 min. Repeat this process with the remaining asparagus bundles.
4. Remove the bundles and allow to cool on a wire rack for 5 min before serving.

Nutrition: Calories 40; Fat 3 g; Carbohydrates 5g; Protein 12 g; Fibre 3 g; Sugar 2 g

MASHED POTATO PANCAKES

5 minutes

15 minutes

6

INGREDIENTS

- 250 g Mashed Potatoes
- 100 g cheddar cheese
- 1 green onion chopped
- 2 strips of cooked bacon
- 1 egg
- 2 tbsp flour
- 100 g panko bread crumbs
- Salt and Pepper to taste

DIRECTIONS

1. Mix Potatoes, egg, cheese,bacon, green onion, and flour
2. Make into a patty form.
3. Coat in panko bread crumbs
4. Place in the freezer for 10 minutes to hold form.
5. Place foil over your rack on your air fryer
6. Cook on 200 C for 10 minutes
7. Flip over and cook for an additional 5 minutes.

Serving Suggestions: Garnish with chopped green onions.

Prep & Cooking Tips: Use large Russet potatoes.

Nutrition: Calories: 273; Total Fat: 13g; Carbohydrates: 28g; Fiber: 2g; Sugar: 2g; Protein: 11g

BAKED POTATOES

20 minutes

45 minutes

6

INGREDIENTS

- 6 potatoes
- 1 tbsp olive oil
- Salt to taste
- 130 grams butter
- 65 ml milk
- 65 grams sour cream
- 65 grams cheddar, shredded and divided

DIRECTIONS

1. Poke the potatoes using a fork.
2. Add to the air fryer.
3. Set it to bake.
4. Cook at 200 degs C for 40 min.
5. Take out of the oven.
6. Slice the potato in half
7. Scoop out the potato flesh.
8. Mix potato flesh with the remaining ingredients.
9. Put the mixture back to the potato shells.
10. Bake in the air fryer for 5 min.

Serving Suggestions: Garnish with chopped green onions.

Prep & Cooking Tips: Use large Russet potatoes.

Nutrition: Calories 487; Fat 19 g; Carbohydrates 65 g; Protein 15 g; Fibre 7.5 g; Sugar 3 g

YORKSHIRE PUDDINGS

1 hour

18 minutes

4

INGREDIENTS

- 1 egg
- 4 tbsp (70 g) flour
- 4 tbsp (80 ml) milk
- 4 tbsp (80 ml) water
- 1/4 tsp salt

DIRECTIONS

1. Mix well all the ingredients together; you need to obtain a smooth batter with no lumps
2. Once the batter is ready, refrigerate for 30 to 60 minutes
3. Preheat the air fryer to 200 C
4. Grease a ramekin with some butter, then add a tsp of oil; heat at 200C in the air fryer for five minutes. This operation will prevent the batter from sticking
5. Once the ramekins are hot, add five tablespoons of Yorkshire Pudding mixture to each one
6. Cook at 200 C for 18 minutes
7. Do not open the air fryer while cooking!

Nutrition: Calories 89; Fat 2 g; Protein 4 g; Carbs 13 g; Fiber 2 g; Sugar 1 g

GOLDEN ASPARAGUS FRITTATA

5 minutes

25 minutes

2-4

INGREDIENTS

- 130 grams asparagus spears, cut into 2.5 cm pieces
- 1 tsp vegetable oil
- 1 tbsp milk
- 6 eggs, beaten
- 60 grams of goat cheese, crumbled
- 1 tbsp minced chives, optional
- Kosher salt and pepper, to taste

DIRECTIONS

1. Add the asparagus spears to a small bowl and drizzle with the vegetable oil. Toss until well coated and transfer to the air fry basket.
2. Place the basket on the air fry position.
3. Select Air Fry. Set temperature to 200 degs C and set time to 5 min. Flip the asparagus halfway through.
4. When cooking is complete, the asparagus should be tender and slightly wilted.
5. Remove the asparagus from the air fryer grill to a baking pan.
6. Stir together the milk and eggs in a medium bowl. Pour the mixture over the asparagus in the pan. Sprinkle with the goat cheese and the chives (if using) over the eggs. Season with salt and pepper.
7. Place the pan on the bake position.
8. Select Bake, set temperature to 160 degs C and set time to 20 min.
9. When cooking is complete, the top should be golden and the eggs should be set.
10. Transfer to a serving dish. Slice and serve.

Nutrition: Calories 370; Fat 25 g; Carbohydrates 4 g; Sugar 0.6 g; Protein 27 g; Fibre 1 g

CHAPTER 3: POULTRY RECIPES

CHICKEN DRUMSTICKS WITH BARBECUE SAUCE

5 minutes

18 minutes

5

INGREDIENTS

- 1 tbsp olive oil
- 10 chicken drumsticks
- Chicken seasoning or rub, to taste
- Salt and ground black pepper, to taste
- 130 grams barbecue sauce
- 30 grams honey

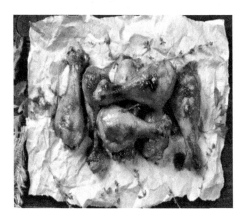

DIRECTIONS

1. Grease the air fry basket with olive oil.
2. Season the chicken thighs with chicken seasoning or rub, salt and pepper.
3. Arrange the chicken drumsticks in the air fry basket.
4. Place the basket on the air fry position.
5. Select Air Fry. Set temperature to 199 degs C and set time to 18 min. Flip the drumsticks halfway through.
6. When cooking is complete, the drumsticks should be lightly browned.
7. Meanwhile, combine the honey and barbecue sauce in a small bowl. Stir to mix well.
8. Remove the drumsticks from the air fryer grill and baste with the sauce mixture to serve.

Nutrition: Calories 338; Fat 28 g; Carbohydrates 11.5 g; Protein 9 g; Fibre 0.2 g; Sugar 9.5 g

CHICKEN PARMESAN IN AIR FRYER

10 minutes

14 minutes

4

INGREDIENTS

- 2 large boneless chicken breasts
- Salt
- Freshly ground black pepper
- 40 g plain flour
- 2 large eggs
- 100 g panko bread crumbs
- 25 g freshly grated Parmesan
- 1 tsp. dried oregano
- 1/2 tsp. garlic powder
- 1/2 tsp. chilli flakes
- 240 g marinara/tomato sauce
- 100 g grated mozzarella
- Freshly chopped parsley, for garnish

DIRECTIONS

1. Gently butterfly the chicken, cutting in half widthwise to obtain 4 thin chicken pieces. Season with salt and pepper on both sides.
2. Place the flour in a shallow bowl and season with a large pinch of salt and pepper. Put the eggs in a second bowl and beat them. In a third bowl, mix together the breadcrumbs, parmesan cheese, oregano, garlic powder, and chilli flakes.
3. Working with chicken pieces one at a time, coat them in flour, then dip them in the eggs and finally press them into the panko mixture, being careful to coat both sides well.
4. Working in batches as needed, place the chicken in the basket and air fry at 200°C for 5 minutes per side. Top chicken with sauce and mozzarella and cook at 200°C for a further 3 minutes or until cheese is melted and golden.
5. Garnish with parsley to serve.

Nutrition: Calories: 419.5; Fat: 16 g; Protein: 30 g; Carbs: 32 g; Fibre: 3 g; Sugar: 10 g

AIR FRYER CHICKEN NUGGETS

5 minutes

15 minutes

4

INGREDIENTS

- 30 g whole wheat flour
- 1/4 tsp salt, or to taste
- 1/4 teaspoon black pepper
- 1 large egg
- 70 g whole wheat panko breadcrumbs
- 35 g grated Parmesan cheese
- 2 teaspoons dried parsley flakes
- 450 grams of boneless, skinless chicken breasts, cut into 2,5 cm cubes
- Olive oil spray

Optional dipping sauce:

- marinara or pizza sauce, barbecue sauce, or ranch dressing

DIRECTIONS

1. Preheat air fryer at 200 degs C for 8-10 min.
2. Set out three small shallow bowls. In the first bowl, place flour, salt, and pepper; mix lightly. In the second bowl, add egg and beat lightly.
3. In the third bowl, combine panko, parmesan cheese, and parsley flakes.
4. One at a time, coat chicken pieces in the flour mixture, then dip into the beaten egg, and finally coat with the panko mixture, pressing lightly to help the coating adhere.
5. Place chicken nuggets in basket of air fryer, in a single layer. Spray the nuggets with olive oil spray (this helps them get golden brown and crispy). You will not be able to cook them all at once.
6. Cook each batch of chicken nuggets for 7 min, or until internal temperature reaches 74 degs C. Do not overcook.

Nutrition: Calories 256; Fat 5.5 g; Carbohydrates 16 g; Protein 33 g; Fibre 1.2 g; Sugar 1 g

CHICKEN BREASTS WITH SPICES

10 minutes

20 minutes

1

INGREDIENTS

- 1 chicken breast (increase accordingly)
- 1/2 tbsp olive oil
- 1/2 tsp salt
- 1/2 tsp pepper
- 1/2 tsp garlic powder (or seasoning of your choice)

DIRECTIONS

1. Preheat the air fryer to 180°C.
2. Grease or spray each chicken breast with oil. Season one side (smooth side) of the chicken breast.
3. Place the chicken breast (smooth side down) in the basket of the air fryer. Season the other side. Set the timer for 10 minutes. After 10 minutes, turn the chicken breast over so that it is cooked on both sides.
4. Check whether the chicken is fully cooked - use a meat thermometer if necessary. Allow the chicken to rest for 5 minutes before serving or slicing.

Nutrition: Calories: 266; Fat: 11 g; Carbohydrates: 2 g; Fibre: 0 g; Sugar: 0 g; Protein: 38 g

SPICED BREADED CHICKEN CUTLETS

5 minutes

11 minutes

2

INGREDIENTS

- 230 grams of boneless, skinless chicken breasts, horizontally sliced in half, into cutlets
- 1/2 tbsp extra-virgin olive oil
- 15 grams breadcrumbs
- 1/4 tsp sea salt
- 1/4 tsp freshly ground black pepper
- 1/4 tsp paprika
- 1/4 tsp garlic powder
- 1/8 tsp onion powder

DIRECTIONS

1. Place the crisper tray on the air fry position. Select Air Fry, temperature to 191 degs C, and set the time to 11 min.
2. Brush each side with the oil.
3. Combine the breadcrumbs, salt, pepper, paprika, garlic powder, and onion powder in a medium shallow bowl. Dredge the chicken cutlets in the bread crumb mixture, turning several times, to ensure the chicken is fully coated.
4. Place the chicken in the crisper tray. Air fry for 9 min. Cooking is done when the internal temperature reaches at least 74 degs C on a food thermometer. If needed Air fry for up to 2 min more.
5. Remove the chicken cutlets and serve immediately.

Nutrition: Calories 216; Fat 7 g; Carbohydrates 7.5 g; Protein 29 g; Fibre 0 g; Sugar 0.5 g

PESTO CHICKEN

10 minutes

20 minutes

2

INGREDIENTS

- 4 chicken drumsticks
- 6 garlic cloves
- 1/2 jalapeno pepper
- 2 tbsp. lemon juice
- 2 tbsp. olive oil
- 1 tbsp. ginger, sliced
- 65 grams coriander
- 1 tsp. salt

DIRECTIONS

1. Add all the ingredients except chicken into the blender and blend until smooth.
2. Pour blended mixture into the large bowl.
3. Add chicken and stir well to coat. Place in refrigerator for 2 hours.
4. Spray air fryer basket with cooking spray.
5. Place marinated chicken into the air fryer basket and cook at 200 degs C for 20 min. Turn halfway through.
6. Serve and enjoy.

Nutrition: Calories 305; Fat 19 g; Carbohydrates 5 g; Sugar 0.7 g; Protein 25 g

MAPLE-TERIYAKI CHICKEN WINGS

5 minutes

14 minutes

4

INGREDIENTS

- 130 grams maple syrup
- 40 grams soy sauce
- 30 grams teriyaki sauce
- 3 garlic cloves, minced
- 2 tsps garlic powder
- 2 tsps onion powder
- 1 tsp freshly ground black pepper
- 900 grams of bone-in chicken wings (drumettes and flats)

DIRECTIONS

1. Place the grill plate on the grill position. Select Grill, set the temperature to 177 degs C, and set the time to 14 min.
2. Meanwhile, in a large bowl, whisk the maple syrup, soy sauce, teriyaki sauce, garlic, garlic powder, onion powder, and black pepper. Add the wings and use tongs to toss and coat.
3. Place the chicken wings on the grill plate. Grill for 5 min. After 5 min, flip the wings and grill for an additional 5 min.
4. Check the wings for doneness. Cooking is done when the internal temperature reaches at minimum 74 degs C on a food thermometer. If needed, grill for up to 4 min more.
5. Remove from the grill and serve.

Nutrition: Calories 559; Fat 29 g; Carbohydrates 41.5 g; Protein 39.3 g; Fibre 0 g; Sugar 37.5 g

BUTTERMILK MARINATED CHICKEN WINGS

1 hour 20 minutes

17 to 19 minutes

4

INGREDIENTS

- 900 grams of chicken wings

Marinade:

- 130 grams buttermilk
- 1/2 tsp salt
- 1/2 tsp black pepper

Coating:

- 130 grams flour
- 130 grams panko breadcrumbs
- 2 tbsp poultry seasoning
- 2 tsps. salt
- Cooking Spray

DIRECTIONS

1. Get a bowl and mix together all the ingredients for the marinade.
2. Dip the chicken wings in the bowl with the marinade and let them rest in the refrigerator for at least an hour (the more they marinate, the tastier they will be).
3. Spritz the crisper tray with cooking spray.
4. Place the crisper tray on the air fry position. Select Air Fry, set the temperature to 182 degs C, and set the time to 19 min.
5. Get a deep bowl and add all the ingredients for the coating by giving it a stir.
6. Remove the chicken wings from the bowl and let the excess marinade drip off. Once done bread them in the coating mixture.
7. Place the chicken wings in the crisper tray in a single layer. Mist the wings with cooking spray. You'll need to work in batches to avoid overcrowding.
8. Air fry for 17 to 19 min, or until the wings are crisp and golden brown on the outside. Flip the wings halfway through the cooking time.
9. Remove from the crisper tray to a plate and repeat with the remaining wings.
10. Serve hot.

Nutrition: Calories 773; Fat 34 g; Carbohydrates 53 g; Protein 60 g; Fibre 4 g; Sugar 16 g

CURRY CHICKEN WITH SWEET POTATO

10 minutes

20 minutes

4

INGREDIENTS

- 455 grams of boneless, skinless chicken thighs
- 1 tsp kosher salt, divided
- 30 grams unsalted butter, melted
- 1 tbsp curry powder
- 2 medium sweet potatoes, peeled and cut in 2.5 cm cubes
- 340 grams of Brussels sprouts, halved

DIRECTIONS

1. Sprinkle the chicken thighs with 1/2 tsp of kosher salt. Place them in the single layer on a baking pan.
2. In a small bowl, stir together the butter and curry powder.
3. Place the sweet potatoes and Brussels sprouts in a large bowl. Drizzle half the curry butter over the vegetables and add the remaining kosher salt. Toss to coat. Transfer the vegetables to the baking pan and place in a single layer around the chicken. Brush half of the remaining curry butter over the chicken.
4. Place the pan on the toast position.
5. Select Toast, set temperature to 200 degs C, and set time to 20 min.
6. After 10 min, remove the pan from the air fryer grill and turn over the chicken thighs. Baste them with the remaining curry butter. Return the pan to the air fryer grill and continue cooking.
7. Cooking is complete when the sweet potatoes are tender, and the chicken is cooked through and reads 74 degs C on a meat thermometer.

Nutrition: Calories 364; Fat 19 g; Carbohydrates 23.5 g; Protein 24.3 g; Fibre 4.8 g; Sugar 7 g

SIMPLE PORK CHOPS

5 minutes

12 minutes

1

INGREDIENTS

- 1 pork chop
- 1/2 tbsp olive oil
- 1/2 tbsp seasoning (BBQ, Curried, Garlic and Herb, Peri Peri etc...)

DIRECTIONS

1. Preheat your air fryer to 200°C.
2. Brush both sides of the pork chop with oil. Add spices and massage evenly.
3. Place the pork chop in your air fryer and set timer for 12 minutes. Flip it after 6 minutes.
4. Make sure the pork chop is fully cooked. The outside should be golden brown and the juices should be clear.

Nutrition: Calories: 629; Fat: 45 g; Protein: 51 g; Carbs: 0 g; Fibre: 0 g; Sugar: 0 g

STEAK IN AIR FRYER

5 minutes

8 minutes

1

INGREDIENTS

- Sirloin steak (or the cut you prefer)
- Oil (optional)
- Pepper and Salt

DIRECTIONS

1. Remove the steak from the refrigerator and leave it at room temperature for at least 30 minutes.
2. Preheat your air fryer to 200 °C. If desired, rub both sides of the steak with a little oil. Place the steak in the air fryer - on the trivet or directly on the bottom of the air fryer basket.
3. Set the timer to the desired time, depending on how well you want it cooked. Flip the steak halfway through. At the end of the cooking time, check to see if the steak is to your liking, remove it from the air fryer and let it rest for at least 5 minutes.

Nutrition: Calories: 331; Fat: 26 g; Carbohydrates: 0 g; Fibre: 0 g; Sugar: 0 g; Protein: 23 g

FAST PORK MEATBALLS WITH RED CHILI

5 minutes

15 minutes

4

INGREDIENTS

- 455 grams of ground pork
- 2 cloves garlic, finely minced
- 130 grams scallions, finely chopped
- 1 1/2 tbsp Worcestershire sauce
- 1/2 tsp freshly grated ginger root
- 1 tsp turmeric powder
- 1 tbsp oyster sauce
- 1 small sliced red chili, for garnish
- Cooking Spray

DIRECTIONS

1. Spritz the air fry basket with cooking spray.
2. Put all the ingredients, except for the red chili in a large bowl. Toss to mix well.
3. Shape the mixture into equally sized balls, then arrange them in the air fry basket and spritz with cooking spray.
4. Place the basket on the air fry position.
5. Select Air Fry. Set temperature to 180 degs C and set time to 15 min.
6. After 7 min, remove the basket from the air fryer grill. Flip the balls. Return the basket to the air fryer grill and continue cooking.
7. When cooking is complete, the balls should be lightly browned.
8. Serve the pork meatballs with red chili on top.

Nutrition: Calories 307; Fat 24 g; Carbohydrates 2.5 g; Protein 19 g; Fibre 0.5 g; Sugar 0.8 g

BEEF WELLINGTON

15 minutes

35 minutes

8

INGREDIENTS

- 1kg beef fillet (one large piece)
- Chicken pate
- 2 sheets of shortcrust pastry
- 1 egg, beaten
- Salt
- Pepper

DIRECTIONS

1. Season the beef with salt, pepper and wrap tightly in cling film
2. Place the beef in the refrigerator for at least one hour
3. Roll out the pastry and brush the edges with the beaten egg
4. Spread the pate over the pastry, making sure it is distributed equally
5. Take now the beef out of the refrigerator and remove the cling film
6. Place the beef in the middle of your pastry
7. Wrap your pastry around the meat and seal the edges with a fork
8. Place in the Air Fryer and cook at 160°C for 35 minutes

Nutrition: Calories: 509; Fat: 28 g; Protein: 34 g; Carbs: 28 g; Fibre: 1 g; Sugar: 0.5 g

PORK, SQUASH, AND PEPPER KEBABS

1 hour 20 minutes

8 minutes

4

INGREDIENTS

For the Pork:
- 455 grams of pork steak, cut into cubes
- 1 tbsp white wine vinegar
- 3 tbsp steak sauce
- 30 grams soy sauce
- 1 tsp powdered chili
- 1 tsp red chili flakes
- 2 tsps smoked paprika
- 1 tsp garlic salt

For the Vegetable:
- 1 green squash, deseeded and cut into cubes
- 1 yellow squash, deseeded and cut into cubes
- 1 red pepper, cut into cubes
- 1 green pepper, cut into cubes
- Salt and ground black pepper, to taste
- Cooking Spray

Special Equipment:
- 4 bamboo skewers, soaked in water for at least 30 min

DIRECTIONS

1. Combine the ingredients for the pork in a large bowl. Press the pork to dunk in the marinade. Wrap the bowl in plastic and let it rest in the refrigerator for at least an hour.
2. Spritz the air fry basket with cooking spray.
3. Remove the pork from the marinade and run the skewers through the pork and vegetables alternatively. Sprinkle with salt and pepper to taste.
4. Arrange the skewers in the pan and spritz with cooking spray.
5. Place the basket on the air fry position.
6. Select Air Fry. Set temperature to 193 degs C and set time to 8 min.
7. After 4 min, remove the basket from the air fryer grill. Flip the skewers. Return the basket to the air fryer grill and continue cooking.
8. When cooking is complete, the pork should be browned, and the vegetables should be lightly charred and tender.
9. Serve immediately.

Nutrition: Calories 240; Fat 13.5 g; Carbohydrates 5 g; Protein 20 g; Fibre 0.8 g; Sugar 3 g

COTTAGE PIE

15 minutes

40 minutes

4

INGREDIENTS

For the base:
- 300g minced beef
- 4 tbsp onions (coarsely diced)
- 2 tbsp carrots (coarsely diced)
- 4 mushrooms (soaked & diced)
- 4 cloves garlic (minced)
- 1 tsp dried mixed herbs
- 2 bay leaves
- 150 ml beef stock
- 1 tbsp Bovril
- 1 tsp ground black pepper
- 2 tbsp plain flour
- 30g butter

For the potato topping:
- 400g potatoes (quartered)
- 130 ml milk
- 2 tbsp butter
- Pinch of salt

Final egg wash topping:
- 1 egg yolk (beaten)

DIRECTIONS

1. Add 1 teaspoon of salt to a saucepan of water and bring to a boil before adding the potatoes. Cook the potatoes until very tender(15-17 minutes).
2. Melt the butter on the baking tray while preheating the fryer. Everything is prepared on the baking tray at 180 degrees C for this recipe.
3. Fry the onion for 1 minute, then add the garlic and fry for another minute until fragrant.
4. Add the ground beef, carrots, mushrooms, herb mix, black pepper, and bay leaves, mix well and cook for 20 minutes. Stir well every 5 minutes.
5. After 10 minutes, add Bovril and beef broth and stir. Continue stirring every 5 minutes.
6. Sprinkle all-purpose flour into the mixture and mix well 2-3 minutes before the end of the cooking time.
7. Hold the baking tray in the air fryer (to keep it warm) while you mash the potatoes.
8. Add the butter, salt, and milk (a little at a time) to the potatoes, mash, and mix well.
9. Spread mashed potatoes over the meat mixture, leveling with the back of a spoon.
10. Use a fork to draw lines across mashed potatoes, then pour the egg yolk on top.
11. Return the baking tray to the air fryer and cook at 180°C for 20 minutes.
12. Serve warm

Nutrition: Calories 360; Fat 22 g; Protein 19 g; Carbs 20 g; Fibre 2.5 g; Sugar 3 g

ROAST BEEF

5 minutes

35 minutes

8

INGREDIENTS

- 1 Kg Beef Roast (up to 1.5 Kg)
- 1 tbsp Olive Oil
- Seasoning to taste

DIRECTIONS

1. Tie the roast to make it more compact
2. Rub the roast with oil
3. Add any seasonings you like
4. Place the beef in the air fryer basket
5. Air fry at 180°C for about 15 minutes per half of Kg (for medium rare beef).
6. Let the roast rest for 5 minutes and serve

Notes

Rare: 46 to 49°C (50 final temperature)

Medium-Rare: 50 to 55°C (58 final temperature)

Medium: 58 to 60°C (63 final temperature)

Medium-Well: 60 to 63°F (65 final temperature)

Well-Done: 65 to 69°F (72 final temperature)

Nutrition: Calories: 443; Fat: 29 g; Carbohydrates: 0 g; Fibre: 0 g; Sugar: 0 g; Protein: 43 g;

LAMB RIBS WITH FRESH MINT

 5 minutes

 18 minutes

 4

INGREDIENTS

- 2 tbsp mustard
- 455 grams of lamb ribs
- 1 tsp rosemary, chopped
- Salt and ground black pepper, to taste
- 30 grams mint leaves, chopped
- 130 ml Greek yogurt

DIRECTIONS

1. Place the crisper tray on the air fry position. Select Air Fry, set the temperature to 177 degs C and set the time to 18 min.
2. Use a brush to apply the mustard to the lamb ribs, and season with rosemary, salt, and pepper. Transfer to the crisper tray.
3. Air fry for 18 min.
4. Meanwhile, combine the mint leaves and yogurt in a bowl.
5. Remove the lamb ribs from the grill when cooked and serve with the mint yogurt.

Nutrition: Calories 413; Fat 35.5 g; Carbohydrates 2.3 g; Protein 19.5 g; Fibre 0.2 g; Sugar 1.2 g

BALSAMIC LONDON BROIL

15 minutes

25 minutes

8

INGREDIENTS

- 900 grams of London broil
- 3 large garlic cloves, minced
- 3 tbsp balsamic vinegar
- 3 tbsp whole-grain mustard
- 2 tbsp olive oil
- Sea salt and ground black pepper, to taste
- 1/2 tsps dried hot red pepper flakes

DIRECTIONS

1. Wash and dry the London broil. Score its sides with a knife.
2. Mix the remaining ingredients. Rub this mixture into the broil, coating it well. Allow marinating for a minimum of 3 hours.
3. Place the crisper tray on the air fry position. Select Air Fry, set the temperature to 200 degs C and set the time to 25 min.
4. Place the meat in the crisper tray. Air fry for 15 min. Turn it over and air fry for an additional 10 min before serving.

Nutrition: Calories 198; Fat 6.2 g; Carbohydrates 0.7 g; Protein 35 g; Fibre 0.25 g; Sugar 0.1 g

ITALIAN PORK MEATBALLS

15 minutes

10 minutes

4

INGREDIENTS

- 340 grams of ground pork
- 60 grams of Parmesan, grated
- 1 tsp Italian seasonings
- 1 tsp ground black pepper
- 1 tsp chili flakes
- 1 tsp fresh parsley, chopped
- 1 tsp avocado oil
- 1 tsp salt

DIRECTIONS

1. Mix up ground pork, Parmesan, Italian seasoning, ground black pepper, chili flakes, parsley, and salt. Make 4 balls from the mixture. Preheat the air fryer to 185 degs C. Then brush the air fryer basket with avocado oil.
2. Put the pork balls inside. Cook them at 185 degs C for 10 minutes.

Nutrition: Calories: 174; Fat: 6.6g; Fibre: 0.2g; Carbs: 1.1g; Protein:26.9g

SALMON FILLET WITH TOMATOES

10 minutes

15 minutes

4

INGREDIENTS

- 680 grams of salmon fillets, patted dry
- 1 tsp kosher salt, divided
- 2 pints cherry or grape tomatoes, halved if large, divided
- 3 tbsp extra-virgin olive oil, divided
- 2 garlic cloves, minced
- 1 small red bell pepper, deseeded and chopped
- 2 tbsp chopped fresh basil, divided

DIRECTIONS

1. Season both sides of the salmon with 1/2 tsp of kosher salt.
2. Put about half of the tomatoes in a large bowl, along with 2 tbsp of olive oil, the remaining 1/2 tsp of kosher salt, bell pepper, garlic, and 1 tbsp of basil. Toss to coat and then transfer to the sheet pan.
3. Arrange the salmon fillets on the sheet pan, skin-side down. Brush them with the remaining 1 tbsp of olive oil.
4. Place the pan on the toast position.
5. Select Toast, set temperature to 190 degs C, and set time to 15 min.
6. After 7 min, remove the pan and fold in the remaining tomatoes. Return the pan to the air fryer grill and continue cooking.
7. When cooked, remove the pan from the air fryer grill. Serve sprinkled with the remaining 1 tbsp of basil.

Nutrition: Calories 312; Fat 19.5 g; Carbohydrates 2.3 g; Protein 30.3 g; Fibre 0.3 g; Sugar 1.8 g

GOLDEN TUNA LETTUCE WRAPS

10 minutes

4-7 minutes

4

INGREDIENTS

- 455 grams of fresh tuna steak, cut into 2.5 cm cubes
- 2 garlic cloves, minced
- 1 tbsp grated fresh ginger
- 1⁄2 tsp toasted sesame oil
- 4 low-sodium whole-wheat tortillas
- 255 grams shredded romaine lettuce
- 1 red bell pepper, thinly sliced
- 30 grams low-fat mayonnaise

DIRECTIONS

1. Combine the tuna cubes, ginger, garlic, and sesame oil in a medium bowl and toss until well coated. Allow sitting for 10 min.
2. When ready, place the tuna cubes in the air fry basket.
3. Place the basket on the air fry position.
4. Select Air Fry, set temp to 199 degs C, and set time to 6 min.
5. When cooking is complete, the tuna cubes should be cooked through and golden brown. Remove the tuna cubes from the air fryer grill to a plate.
6. Make the wraps: Place the tortillas on a flat surface and top each tortilla evenly with the cooked tuna, lettuce, bell pepper, and finish with the mayonnaise. Roll them up and serve immediately.

Nutrition: Calories 292; Fat 14 g; Carbohydrates 12 g; Protein 27.3 g; Fibre 1.3 g; Sugar 0 g

GOLD SALMON PATTIES

5 minutes

13 minutes

6 patties

INGREDIENTS

- 420 grams of can pink salmon, drained and bones removed
- 65 grams breadcrumbs
- 1 egg, whisked
- 2 scallions, diced
- 1 tsp garlic powder
- Salt and pepper, to taste
- Cooking Spray

DIRECTIONS

1. Stir together the salmon, breadcrumbs, whisked egg, garlic powder, scallions, salt, and pepper in a large bowl until well incorporated.
2. Divide the salmon mixture into six equal portions and form each into a patty with your hands.
3. Arrange the salmon patties in the air fry basket and spritz them with cooking spray.
4. Place the basket on the air fry position.
5. Air Fry, set the temperature to 200 degs C, and set time to 12 min. Flip the patties once halfway through.
6. When cooking is complete, the patties should be golden brown and cooked through. Remove the patties from the air fryer grill and serve on a plate.

Nutrition: Calories 142; Fat 7.8 g; Carbohydrates 9.5 g; Protein 23 g; Fibre 0.5 g; Sugar 0.8 g

CRISPY FISH STICKS

10 minutes

10 minutes

4

INGREDIENTS

- 455 grams of cod fillets
- 30 grams all-purpose flour
- 1 large egg
- 1 tsp Dijon mustard
- 65 grams breadcrumbs
- 1 tbsp dried parsley
- 1 tsp paprika
- 1/2 tsp freshly ground black pepper
- Non-stick cooking spray

DIRECTIONS

1. Place the crisper tray on the air fry position. Select Air Fry, set the temperature to 199 degs C, and set the time to 10 min.
2. Cut the fish fillets into 19 - to 25-mm-wide strips.
3. Place the flour on a plate. In a medium shallow bowl, whisk together the egg and Dijon mustard. In a separate medium shallow bowl, combine the breadcrumbs, dried parsley, paprika, and black pepper.
4. One at a time, dredge the cod strips in the flour, shaking off any excess, then coat them in the egg mixture. Finally, dredge them in the bread crumb mixture and coat on all sides.
5. Spray the crisper tray with the cooking spray. Place the cod fillet strips in the crisper tray, and coat them with the cooking spray. Air fry for 10 min.
6. Remove the fish sticks from the crisper tray and serve.

Nutrition: Calories 187; Fat 2.5 g; Carbohydrates 13.5 g; Protein 24.5 g; Fibre 1 g; Sugar 0.8 g

PANKO-CRUSTED CATFISH NUGGETS

 10 minutes

 7-8 minutes

 4

INGREDIENTS

- 2 medium catfish fillets, cut into chunks (approximately 5 cm)
- Salt and pepper, to taste
- 2 eggs
- 2 tbsp skim milk
- 65 grams corn-starch
- 130 grams panko breadcrumbs
- Cooking Spray

DIRECTIONS

1. In a medium bowl, season the fish chunks with salt and pepper to taste.
2. In a small bowl, beat together the eggs with milk until well combined.
3. Place the corn-starch and breadcrumbs into separate shallow dishes.
4. Dredge the fish chunks one at a time in the corn-starch, coating well on both sides, then dip in the egg mixture, shaking off any excess, finally press well into the bread crumbs. Spritz the fish chunks with cooking spray.
5. Arrange the fish chunks in the air fry basket in a single layer.
6. Place the basket on the air fry position.
7. Select Air Fry, set the temperature to 199 degs C, and set time to 8 min. Flip the fish chunks halfway through the cooking time.
8. When cooking is complete, they should be no longer translucent in the centre and golden brown. Remove the fish chunks from the air fryer grill to a plate. Serve warm.

Nutrition: Calories 310; Fat 7.8 g; Carbohydrates 34 g; Protein 22.5 g; Fibre 1 g; Sugar 1.5 g

PANKO SCALLOPS

5 minutes

7 minutes

4

INGREDIENTS

- 1 egg
- 3 tbsp flour
- 130 grams breadcrumbs
- 455 grams of fresh scallops
- 2 tbsp olive oil
- Salt and black pepper, to taste

DIRECTIONS

1. In a bowl, lightly beat the egg. Place the flour and breadcrumbs into separate shallow dishes.
2. Dredge the scallops in the flour and shake off any excess. Dip the flour-coated scallops in the beaten egg and roll in the breadcrumbs.
3. Brush the scallops generously with olive oil and season with salt and pepper. Transfer the scallops to the air fry basket.
4. Place the basket on the air fry position.
5. Select Air Fry, set temperature to 182 degs C, and set time to 7 min. Flip the scallops halfway through the cooking time.
6. When cooking is complete, the scallops should reach an internal temperature of just 63 degs C on a meat thermometer. Remove the basket from the air fryer grill. Let the scallops cool for 5 min and serve.

Nutrition: Calories 226; Fat 2.7 g; Carbohydrates 26.5 g; Protein 19.5 g; Fibre 1.3 g; Sugar 1.5 g

FRIED SHRIMP WITH MAYONNAISE SAUCE

5 minutes

7 minutes

4

INGREDIENTS

Shrimp:

- 12 jumbo shrimp
- 1/2 tsp garlic salt
- 1/4 tsp freshly cracked mixed peppercorns

Sauce:

- 4 tbsp mayonnaise
- 1 tsp grated lemon rind
- 1 tsp Dijon mustard
- 1 tsp chipotle powder (optional)
- 1/2 tsp cumin powder (optional)

DIRECTIONS

1. Place the crisper tray on the air fry position. Select Air Fry, set the temperature to 200 degs C, and set the time to 8 min.
2. In a medium bowl, season the shrimp with garlic salt and cracked mixed peppercorns.
3. Place the shrimp in the crisper tray. Air fry for 5 min. Flip the shrimp and cook for another 2 min until they are pink and no longer opaque.
4. Meanwhile, stir together all the ingredients for the sauce in a small bowl until well mixed.
5. Remove the shrimp from the crisper tray and serve alongside the sauce.

Nutrition: Calories 152; Fat 6.5 g; Carbohydrates 0 g; Protein 22.5 g; Fibre 0 g; Sugar 0 g

SHRIMP SALAD WITH CAESAR DRESSING

10 minutes   15 minutes   4

INGREDIENTS

- 1/2 baguette, cut into 2.5 cm cubes (about 265 grams)
- 4 tbsp extra-virgin olive oil, divided
- 1/4 tsp granulated garlic
- 1/4 tsp kosher salt
- 95 grams Caesar dressing, divided
- 2 romaine lettuce hearts, cut in half lengthwise and ends trimmed
- 455 grams of medium shrimp, peeled and deveined
- 60 grams of Parmesan cheese, coarsely grated

DIRECTIONS

1. Make the croutons: Put the bread cubes in a medium bowl and drizzle 3 tbsp of olive oil over top. Season with salt and granulated garlic and toss to coat. Transfer to the air fry basket in a single layer.
2. Place the basket on the air fry position.
3. Select Air Fry, set temperature to 200 degs C, and set time to 4 min. Toss the croutons halfway through the cooking time.
4. When done, remove the air fry basket from the air fryer grill and set aside.
5. Brush 2 tbsp of Caesar dressing on the cut side of the lettuce. Set aside.
6. Toss the shrimp with the 30 grams of Caesar dressing in a large bowl until well coated. Set aside.
7. Coat the sheet pan with the remaining 1 tbsp of olive oil. Arrange the romaine halves on the coated pan, cut side down. Brush the tops with the remaining 2 tbsp of Caesar dressing.
8. Place the pan on the toast position.
9. Select Toast, set temperature to 190 degs C, and set time to 10 min.
10. After 5 min, remove the pan from the air fryer grill and flip the romaine halves. Spoon the shrimp around the lettuce. Return the pan to the air fryer grill and continue cooking.
11. When done, remove the sheet pan from the air fryer grill. If they are not quite cooked through, roast for another 1 minute.
12. On each of four plates, put a romaine half. Divide the shrimp among the plates and top with croutons and grated Parmesan cheese. Serve immediately.

Nutrition: Calories 286; Fat 17.5 g; Carbohydrates 6.8 g; Protein 25.5 g; Fibre 0.8 g; Sugar 0.3 g

BEERY COD FILLET

5 minutes

15 minutes

4

INGREDIENTS

- 2 eggs
- 130 grams malty beer
- 130 grams all-purpose flour
- 65 grams corn-starch
- 1 tsp garlic powder
- Salt and pepper, to taste
- 455 grams of cod fillets
- Cooking Spray

DIRECTIONS

1. In a shallow bowl, beat together the eggs with the beer. In another shallow bowl, thoroughly combine the corn-starch and flour. Sprinkle with salt, garlic powder, and pepper.
2. Dredge each cod fillet in the flour mixture, then in the egg mixture. Dip each piece of fish in the flour mixture a second time.
3. Spritz the air fry basket with cooking spray. Arrange the cod fillets in the basket in a single layer.
4. Place the basket on the air fry position.
5. Select Air Fry, set the temperature to 200 degs C, and set time to 15 min. Flip the fillets halfway through the cooking time.
6. When cooking is complete, the cod should reach an internal temperature of 63 degs C on a meat thermometer and the outside should be crispy. Let the fish cool for 5 min and serve.

Nutrition: Calories 310; Fat 4.8 g; Carbohydrates 33.8 g; Protein 30 g; Fibre 33.8 g; Sugar 0 g

LEMONY CHEESECAKE

5 minutes

25 minutes

6

INGREDIENTS

- 500 grams of ricotta cheese
- 155 grams of sugar
- 3 eggs, beaten
- 3 tbsp flour
- 1 lemon, juiced and zested
- 2 tsps. vanilla extract

DIRECTIONS

1. In a very large mixing bowl, stir all the ingredients until the mixture reaches a creamy consistency.
2. Pour the mixture in a baking pan and place it in the air fryer grill.
3. Place the pan on the bake position.
4. Select Bake, set temperature to 160 degs C, and set time to 25 min.
5. When cooking is complete, a toothpick inserted in the centre should come out clean.
6. Allow to cool for 10 min on a wire rack before serving.

Nutrition: Calories 292.5; Fat 13.3 g; Carbohydrates 29.5 g; Protein 13.3 g; Fibre 0.4 g; Sugar 24.3 g

CHOCOLATE CHIP COOKIES

10 minutes

8 minutes

12

INGREDIENTS

- 115 g butter, melted
- 55 g brown sugar
- 50 g caster sugar
- 1 large egg
- 1 tsp. pure vanilla extract
- 185 g plain flour
- 1/2 tsp. bicarbonate of soda
- 1/2 tsp. salt
- 120 g chocolate chips
- 35 g chopped walnuts

DIRECTIONS

1. In a medium bowl, combine melted butter and sugar. Add the egg and vanilla and beat until incorporated. Add the flour, baking soda, and salt and stir until combined.
2. Place a small piece of parchment in the frying basket, making sure there is room around the edges to allow air circulation. Working in batches, using a large cookie scoop (about 3 tablespoons), scoop the batter onto parchment paper, leaving 5 cm between each cookie. Press down the batter until slightly flattened.
3. Air fry for 8 minutes at 180 °C. The cookies will turn golden brown and slightly soft.
4. Let cool for 5 minutes before serving.

Nutrition: Calories: 220; Fat: 12 g; Protein: 3 g; Carbs: 24 g; Fibre: 2.5 g; Sugar: 11 g

BRITISH VICTORIA SPONGE

15 minutes

28 minutes

8

INGREDIENTS

For the Victoria Sponge:
- 100 g Plain Flour
- 100 g Butter
- 100 g Caster Sugar
- 2 Medium Eggs

For the Cake Filling:
- 2 tbsp. Strawberry Jam
- 50 g Butter
- 100 g Icing Sugar
- 1 tbsp. Whipped Cream

DIRECTIONS

1. Preheat the Air Fryer to 180°C.
2. Grease a baking dish.
3. Cream the sugar and the butter until light and fluffy.
4. Now beat in the eggs, add a little flour with each.
5. Now gently fold in the flour.
6. Arrange your mixture into the tin and cook for 15 minutes, 180°C, then 10 minutes, 170°C.
7. Now leave it to cool and once it is cooled slice into two equal slices of sponge.
8. Now make the filling: Cream the butter, until you have a thick creamy mixture gradually add icing sugar and whipped cream.
9. Arrange a layer of strawberry jam, then a layer of cake filling, then add your other sponge on top.
10. Serve!

Nutrition: Calories: 243; Fat: 16.5 g; Protein: 3 g; Carbs: 21 g; Fibre: 1 g; Sugar: 12 g

CLASSIC POUND CAKE

5 minutes

30 minutes

8

INGREDIENTS

- 1 stick butter, at room temperature
- 130 grams Swerve Sweetener
- 4 eggs
- 190 grams coconut flour
- 65 grams buttermilk
- 1⁄2 tsp baking soda
- 1⁄2 tsp baking powder
- 1⁄4 tsp salt
- 1 tsp vanilla essence
- A pinch of ground star anise
- A pinch of freshly grated nutmeg
- Cooking Spray

DIRECTIONS

1. Place the baking pan on the bake position. Select Bake, set the temperature to 160 degs C, and set the time to 30 min.
2. Spray the baking pan with cooking spray.
3. With an electric or hand mixer, beat butter and Swerve until creamy. One at a time, mix in the eggs and whisk until fluffy. Add now the remaining ones and stir to combine.
4. Transfer the batter to the baking pan. Bake for 30 min until the centre of the cake is springy. Rotate halfway through the cooking time.
5. Let the cake to cool down in the pan for 10 min before removing and serving.

Nutrition: Calories: 155; Fat: 12 g; Fibre: 0 g; Carbs:4 g; Protein:5.6 g; Sugar: 3.6 g

GINGER BISCUITS

10 minutes

16 minutes

10-12

INGREDIENTS

- 270 g plain flour
- 2 tsp ground ginger
- 2 tsp baking soda
- 1 tbsp cinnamon
- ½ tsp salt
- 170 g butter room temperature
- 200 g white sugar
- 1 egg
- 85 g maple syrup
- 70 g sugar for coating the cookies

DIRECTIONS

1. In a large bowl, mix together the flour, ginger, baking soda, cinnamon, and salt.
2. In a second bowl, beat the butter with the sugar, egg, and maple syrup until creamy.
3. Combine the dry ingredients with the wet ones. Once everything is mixed, shape into small balls using your hands.
4. Flat each ball a little (the thicker the better!)
5. Preheat your air fryer at 150°C, and then air fry the cookies for 8 minutes at the same temperature.
6. Add 4-6 biscuits simultaneously (leaving space between each one). It is not necessary to rotate them.
7. Cook until hard on the outside but soft to touch when you press the biscuit.
8. Repeat steps 6-8 for the remaining cookies.
9. Let cool before eating and enjoy!

Nutrition: Calories 300; Fat 14 g; Protein 4 g; Carbs 45 g; Fiber 3 g; Sugar 25 g

GOLDEN BANANAS WITH CHOCOLATE SAUCE

10 minutes

7 minutes

6

INGREDIENTS

- 30 grams corn-starch
- 30 grams plain breadcrumbs
- 1 large egg, beaten
- 3 bananas, halved crosswise
- Cooking Spray
- Chocolate sauce, for serving

DIRECTIONS

1. Place the breadcrumbs, egg, and corn-starch in three separate bowls.
2. Roll the bananas in the corn-starch, then in the beaten egg, and finally in the breadcrumbs to coat well.
3. Spritz the air fry basket with cooking spray.
4. Arrange the banana halves in the air fry basket and mist them with cooking spray.
5. Place the basket on the air fry position.
6. Select Air Fry, set temperature to 180 degs C, and set time to 7 min.
7. After about 5 min, flip the bananas and continue to air fry for another 2 min.
8. When cooking is complete, remove the bananas from the air fryer grill to a serving plate. Serve now with the chocolate sauce drizzled over the top.

Nutrition: Calories 142; Fat 1.2 g; Carbohydrates 32 g; Protein 2.5 g; Fibre 3 g; Sugar 14 g

CHOCOLATE AND CHILLI BROWNIES IN THE AIRFRYER

15 minutes

15-20 minutes

6

INGREDIENTS

- 200 g butter, melted
- 100 g cocoa powder
- 75 g dark chocolate, melted
- 2 large eggs
- 150 g caster sugar
- 1/2 tsp vanilla essence
- 150 g self-raising flour
- 1 level tbsp crushed dried chilli flakes

DIRECTIONS

1. Preheat the air fryer to 180°C
2. Mix the butter, sugar and crushed dried chillies.
3. Beat and mix in the eggs. Add the melted chocolate and vanilla essence.
4. Gradually add the flour and cocoa powder. Mix gently, do not stir too much.
5. Using a greased or baking paper lined tin/container, pour in the mixture.
6. Cook in the air fryer for 15 to 20 minutes, checking periodically to see if the upper part does not burn; If it's cooking quickly, cover it with foil or baking paper.
7. When it's done, let it cool, then cut into smaller portions to serve.

Nutrition: Calories: 300; Fat: 22 g; Protein: 5 g; Carbs: 19 g; Fibre: 5 g; Sugar: 11 g

MUFFINS WITH BLUEBERRIES

25 minutes

15 minutes

3

INGREDIENTS

- 60 grams of butter
- 60 ml of fresh whole milk
- 140 grams of flour type "00"
- 60 grams of sugar
- 1 egg
- 5 grams of baking powder
- 1/2 sachet of vanillin
- 70 grams of blueberries
- 1/4 tsp of baking soda
- 1 pinch of salt

Cooking tools:

- Baking cups for muffins

DIRECTIONS

1. Soften the butter at room temperature in the bowl. Add the sugar and then whisk vigorously until a creamy mixture is obtained.
2. Add the egg while continuing to whip.
3. Pour the milk at room temperature slowly, whipping until smooth.
4. Sift the flour into a bowl and mix it together with the baking powder, baking soda, vanillin, and salt. Add them little by little to the mixture until it is creamy and without lumps.
5. Add the blueberries to the dough.
6. Preheat the air fryer to 185 degs C.
7. Fill the baking cups with the mixture.
8. Put the cups with the dough in the basket and insert them into the air fryer.
9. Set the timer to 15 min and bake the muffins until lightly browned.

Nutrition: Calories 287; Fat 3 g; Carbohydrates 2 g; Sugar 3 g; Protein 11 g

INDEX

Printed in Great Britain
by Amazon

42075945R00044